MORE MARTINI WISDOM

And other midlife

musings from

The Three Tomatoes

Cheryl Benton and Roni Jenkins

the three
tomatoes book publishing

Cover Photo iStock and interior images iStock and Shutterstock.

Cover design: Susan Herbst

Visit our website at www.thethreetomatoes.com

Printed in the United States of America
November, 2020
The Three Tomatoes Book Publishing
6 Soundview Rd.
Glen Cove, New York 11542

ISBN: 978-1-7353585-8-1

Dedication

This book is dedicated to all the fun loving and free-spirited women we know who are fully enjoying life at every age and every stage.

"Shaken, not stirred."

In memory of

Sean Connery, aka "Bond, James Bond."

We enjoy the occasional martini and there's definitely something to be said for viewing midlife and beyond through a martini glass. Our "martini ladies" have been spouting their wisdom— sometimes borrowed, sometimes new— once a week in The Three Tomatoes newsletters for quite some time. When we turned some of them into our first little book, *Martini Wisdom,* we were gratified by the response, so we decided to bring you *More Martini Wisdom*. And in a year that brought us a global pandemic, what helped us get through was a shaken, not stirred martini, laughter with friends, and gratefulness for our loved ones. We hope our little book puts a smile on your face too.

Cheers,

Cheryl Benton and Roni Jenkins
www.thethreetomatoes.com

Martini Wisdom from The Three Tomatoes

Darlings,

I had this dream there was a pandemic and everyone ran out of toilet paper.
Crazy right?

Martini Wisdom from The Three Tomatoes

Darlings,

A day without wine is like...hmmm.

And what day is it anyway?

Martini Wisdom from The Three Tomatoes

Darlings,

Remember: bad boys are fun...until they're not.

Martini Wisdom from The Three Tomatoes

Darlings,

The only thing I remember from chemistry class is that alcohol is a solution.

Martini Wisdom from The Three Tomatoes

Darlings,

Of course size matters!

You're a bigger d*ck today than you were

yesterday.

Martini Wisdom from The Three Tomatoes

Darling Santa,

I was a very good girl this year.

Well most of the time. Okay some of the time.

Oh screw it. I'll buy my own gifts.

Martini Wisdom from The Three Tomatoes

Darlings,

If I wanted someone around all the time,

I'd get a dog.

Martini Wisdom from The Three Tomatoes

Darlings,

I hate being late but I'm so good at it.

Martini Wisdom from The Three Tomatoes

Darlings,

Thought for the day…no woman would ever have declared hair and nail salons non-essential.

Martini Wisdom from The Three Tomatoes

Darlings,

If I wanted to be perfect,
I'd be a martini, not a mere mortal.

Martini Wisdom from The Three Tomatoes

Darlings,

The only thing I'll miss about quarantine

is having to wear a bra again.

Martini Wisdom from The Three Tomatoes

Darlings,

There are better uses for vodka than disinfecting your hands.

Martini Wisdom from The Three Tomatoes

Darlings,

I'm so stressed from adjusting lighting,
backgrounds, hair and makeup for Zoom cocktails,
I need cocktails for my cocktails.

Martini Wisdom from The Three Tomatoes

Darlings,

We need our days of the week panties—they'll remind us what day it is and to change them too.

Martini Wisdom from The Three Tomatoes

Darlings,

If not now, when? Be adventurous, be bold,

have tales to tell.

Martini Wisdom from The Three Tomatoes

Darlings,

When I said, "I *vant* to be alone,"

I didn't mean for months.

Martini Wisdom from The Three Tomatoes

Darlings,

I feel sorry for ladies who *don't* lunch.
They must have that burden of doing important
things.

Martini Wisdom from The Three Tomatoes

Darlings,

Remember: you're the leading character

in your story.

Make her interesting.

Martini Wisdom from The Three Tomatoes

Darlings,

Who needs guys with perfect abs when dad bods
make perfect pillows?

Martini Wisdom from The Three Tomatoes

Darlings,

Life has as many acts as you can create.

The key is to enjoy the play.

Martini Wisdom from The Three Tomatoes

Darlings,

If you count the martini olives as you eat them,

does that count as mindful eating?

Martini Wisdom from The Three Tomatoes

Darlings,

Don't question why.

Just do as I say, and no one gets hurt.

Martini Wisdom from The Three Tomatoes

Darlings,

The best way to avoid touching your face is to have
a glass of wine in each hand.
Problem solved.

Martini Wisdom from The Three Tomatoes

Darlings,

Lose weight, exercise more, meditate.

Oh wait...those were last year's resolutions too.

Martini Wisdom from The Three Tomatoes

Darlings,

Remember how we were worried

we'd run out of vodka?

Oh right, and toilet paper too.

Martini Wisdom from The Three Tomatoes

Darlings,

I still don't understand what a wine stopper is for.

Martini Wisdom from The Three Tomatoes

Darlings,

Another day has gone by and I haven't used
Algebra once.

Martini Wisdom from The Three Tomatoes

Darlings,

When it comes to criticizing our every little flaw,

mirrors are so yesterday.

Doesn't Zoom make it so much easier?

Martini Wisdom from The Three Tomatoes

Darlings,

According to this BMI chart,
I'm too short.

Martini Wisdom from The Three Tomatoes

Darlings,

Those silly passwords are a bore.

I'm using one I'll remember:

shedrinkswine24x7.

Martini Wisdom from The Three Tomatoes

Darlings,

I'm living in a drama free bubble.

It's a champagne bubble, but a bubble,
nonetheless.

Martini Wisdom from The Three Tomatoes

Darlings,

Every day I struggle with whether I want to look good naked or eat chocolate.

Martini Wisdom from The Three Tomatoes

Darlings,

When we can all get together again,

let's not tell some people.

Martini Wisdom from The Three Tomatoes

Darlings,

When life gets you down, just cross

the street to the sunny side.

If that doesn't work, drink wine.

Martini Wisdom from The Three Tomatoes

Darlings,

My life coach is a very dry vodka martini.

Martini Wisdom from The Three Tomatoes

Darlings,

A public service announcement:

Trust me...you can dance.

Love, Vodka

Martini Wisdom from The Three Tomatoes

Darlings,

Have you ever secretly skipped ahead to the next episode of a show you've been watching together? Asking for a friend.

Martini Wisdom from The Three Tomatoes

Darlings,

A good man can make you feel sexy and witty...
Oh wait...that's wine.

Martini Wisdom from The Three Tomatoes

Darlings,

There's a solution to the glass that's half empty…

fill it with wine.

Martini Wisdom from The Three Tomatoes

Darlings,

My favorite part of winter is when it's over.

Then I can start complaining that it's too hot.

Martini Wisdom from The Three Tomatoes

Darlings,

If his idea of romance is camping under the stars,

RUN!

Martini Wisdom from The Three Tomatoes

Darlings,

It's a text message, not an essay.

Martini Wisdom from The Three Tomatoes

Darlings,

Thank goodness for martinis.
How else would we know how funny, witty,
and entertaining we are?

Martini Wisdom from The Three Tomatoes

Darlings,

If you're texting me at six in the morning,
it better be to say you won the lottery
and you're sharing it with me.

Martini Wisdom from The Three Tomatoes

Darlings,

If he starts mansplaining, just say,

"Oh, now I finally get it."

Don't worry, he won't get the sarcasm.

Martini Wisdom from The Three Tomatoes

Darlings,

If you have to ask what time happy hour is,

you're an amateur and we can't be friends.

Martini Wisdom from The Three Tomatoes

Darlings,

Of course, I'm outdoorsy.

I love to drink on yachts.

Martini Wisdom from The Three Tomatoes

Darlings,

If you think you'll regret it in the morning,

sleep until noon.

Problem solved.

Martini Wisdom from The Three Tomatoes

Darlings,

If you have to ask if you look fat in it,

change the damned outfit.

Martini Wisdom from The Three Tomatoes

Darlings,

Sunsets bring magical moments and remind us
that tomorrow we can start anew.

About Us

From the publishers of The Three Tomatoes, a digital lifestyle magazine for women, *Martini Wisdom* and *More Martini Wisdom* are the perfect anecdote to all those motivational and inspirational books about midlife and beyond. It's the inappropriate thought bubbles that the "martini ladies" dare to say out loud. Come on...you know you've had some of these thoughts too. It's the perfect anywhere read and you're going to want to share it with your BFFs too.

The Three Tomatoes mother and daughter duo, Cheryl Benton and Roni Jenkins, are the tomatoes behind Martini Wisdom. Visit us at The Three Tomatoes, www.thethreetomatoes.com PS: If you like the book, please leave a review on Amazon.

Made in United States
Orlando, FL
16 May 2024

46932633R00033